# I Will
# Blow You
# a Kiss

AuthorHouse™
1663 Liberty Drive
Bloomington, IN 47403
www.authorhouse.com
Phone: 833-262-8899

Because of the dynamic nature of the Internet, any web addresses or links contained in this book may have changed since publication and may no longer be valid. The views expressed in this work are solely those of the author and do not necessarily reflect the views of the publisher, and the publisher hereby disclaims any responsibility for them.

Any people depicted in stock imagery provided by Getty Images are models, and such images are being used for illustrative purposes only.
Certain stock imagery © Getty Images.

This book is printed on acid-free paper.

ISBN: 978-1-6655-3951-7 (sc)
978-1-6655-3952-4 (e)

Print information available on the last page.

Published by AuthorHouse  09/25/2021

authorHOUSE

# I Will Blow You a Kiss

**Mary Robertson**

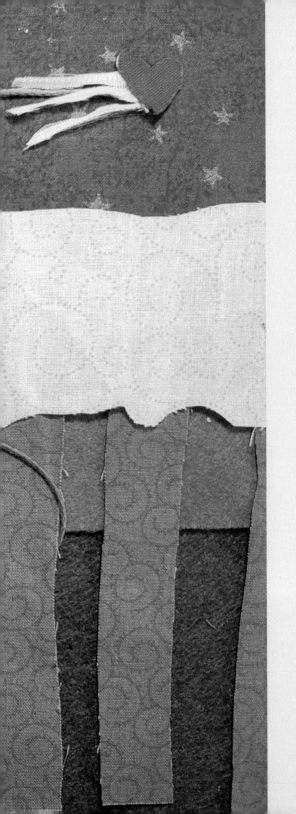

I will blow you a kiss

From far, far away

To find you as you lay,

Dreams tangled in your hair,

Fast asleep, my sweet.

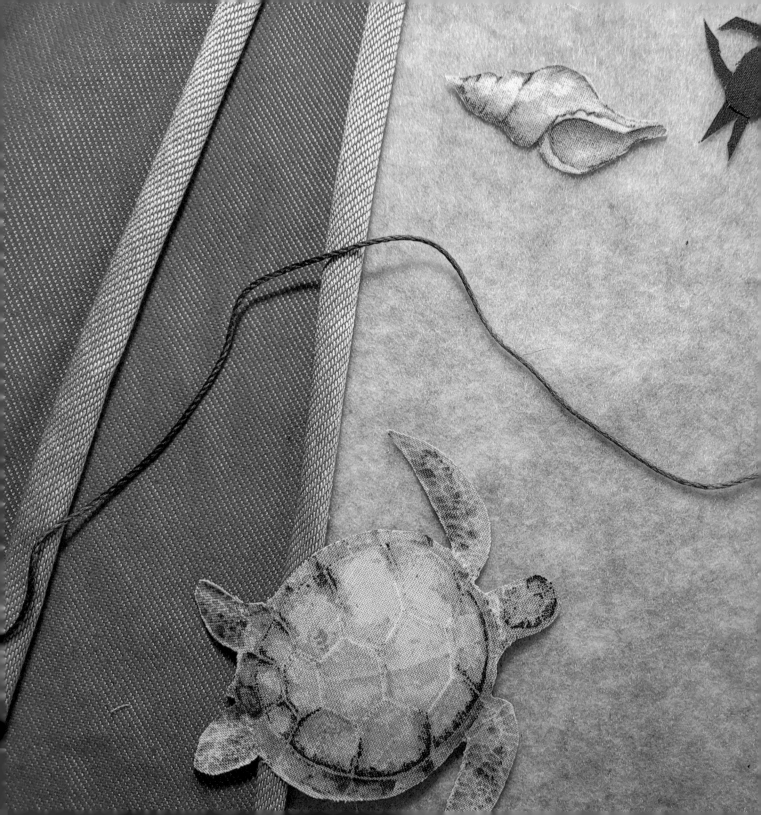

Past the stars

My kiss will fly,

Across lands,

Watching oceans go by.

My kiss will dance on cold,
cold snow

And leap over rivers
and rocks.

Fast, past the farmers with
seed to sow.

But slow, not to wake
birds nesting in the rustling
leaves on the trees

And sleeping river otters,
making ripples in the water.

It will fly through the desert,

So hot in the day,

And ski down a mountain,

Shaking icicles off trees.

When my kiss finds a jungle,

It will climb the highest tree

And leap across treetops

Like a wild monkey.

Into your house, my kiss
it will come,

Gentle and happy, like a
song you might hum.

It will drift through the air,
bringing all my love.

It has come just for you,
my little dove.

And quietly, like a
soft butterfly,

It will land, my little
kiss, when morning
is nigh.

You will wake with
my kiss; though it's
traveled far,

My love will find you
wherever you are.

## About the Author

**Mary** is a young woman living in a small town in New Hampshire where she spends her time working with children and teens, and doting on her nieces and nephews. Mary loves to travel, and always bring home stories of her adventures so that the little ones in her life can dream of a bigger world.

Printed in the United States
by Baker & Taylor Publisher Services